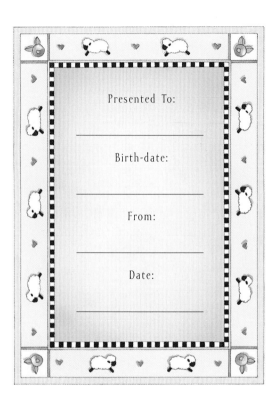

Presented To:

_____

Birth-date:

_____

From:

_____

Date:

_____

Baby's First Bible

Little Stories for Little Hearts

ZONDERKIDZ

Baby's First Bible
Copyright © 1997 by Multnomah Publishing, Inc.
Illustrations © 1997 by Tish Tenud
Copyright © 2000 by Melody Carlson
First published by Zondervan 2002

Requests for information should be addressed to:

Zonderkidz, 3900 Sparks Dr. SE, Grand Rapids, Michigan 49546

ISBN 978-0-310-70448-5

Any Internet addresses (websites, blogs, etc.) and telephone numbers in this book are offered as a resource. They are not intended in any way to be or imply an endorsement by Zondervan, nor does Zondervan vouch for the content of these sites and numbers for the life of this book.

Printed in China

24 /DSC/ 44

Baby's First Bible

Little Stories for Little Hearts

BY MELODY CARLSON

ILLUSTRATED BY TISH TENUD

Contents

◆

$\mathcal{G}$od spoke to the night

"Let there be light!"

And all of the world

Grew sunny and bright.

God said, "I can

Create a man.

And also a woman,

As part of my plan."

Noah made a boat.

And God made it float

When the water covered

The earth like a coat.

Abraham heard God call,

And though he felt small,

He left his homeland

To be father of all.

$\mathcal{R}$ebekah did her part

God knew she was smart.

She gave the camels water

And won Isaac's heart.

$\mathcal{J}$acob went to sleep

And dreamed very deep,

Of angels coming up and down

A stairway tall and steep.

A coat of bright colors

Angered the brothers,

For Jacob loved Joseph

More than the others.

A princess heard a cry

In the river reeds nearby.

She found the baby Moses

And said, "He shall not die!"

$\mathcal{M}$oses, it is Me."

God said, "You will see,

Why I chose you to be the one,

To set my people free."

Moses said, "Let's start,

Now go with all your heart!"

And the people walked in wonder

As God made the waters part.

$\mathcal{J}$oshua, do not fear,"

Said God, "For I am near.

Jericho will tumble

When your horns they hear."

Samson was so strong,

When his hair was very long.

God gave him victory

When he fought against

the throng!

Samuel heard God call,

When he was very small.

Was it truly God's voice?

It was – after all!

When David was a boy.

A harp was his toy.

And when he cared for the sheep,

He sang to God with joy!

Goliath was a sight–

A giant with great might!

But God helped little David

To beat him in a fight.

Solomon was a king.

God said, "Ask for anything."

But Solomon said, "Wisdom

Is all that I'm wanting."

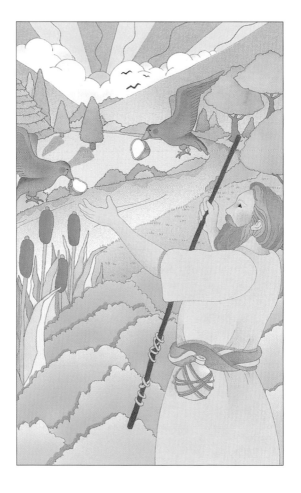

Elijah needed bread,

"I'll care for you," God said.

God sent birds to bring him food,

And Elijah was well fed.

Daniel didn't sin;

He didn't bow to men.

So God closed the lions' mouths

While he was in their den.

Jonah ran away.

He didn't want to obey.

But when he was eaten by a fish,

"I'm sorry, God," he prayed.

The New Testament

An angel said to Mary,

"Fear not, just wait and see,

You will bear God's only Son,

And blessed you will be!"

$\mathcal{L}$ate one starry night,

There was a glorious sight!

Jesus Christ was born on earth,

To shine his Holy Light.

His teachers were surprised,

Young Jesus was so wise.

When He was in his Father's house,

He opened up their eyes.

Down flew a dove,

Sent from above,

When John baptized Jesus

With the Father's love.

Jesus said, "I'll keep

And care for all my sheep.

I'll lead them through the valleys,

And over mountains steep."

$\mathcal{L}$ook how the flowers grow.

They don't weave; they don't sew.

Yet they are so lovely,

See how their colors glow!"

Jesus walked by the sea

Known as Galilee.

Jesus called the fishermen,

"Come and follow me!"

The host ran out of wine,

Wedding guests stood in line.

Then Jesus did a miracle,

And everything was fine!

As the boat crossed the sea,

A wind blew frightfully.

But when Jesus calmed the storm,

His friends said, "Who is He?"

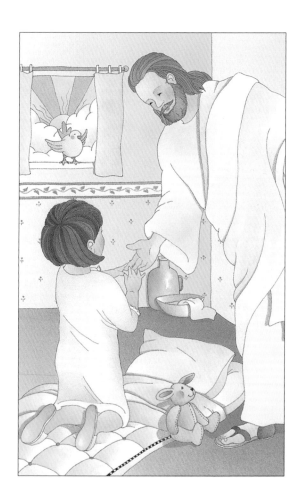

$\mathcal{J}$esus heard his cries:

"My daughter surely dies!"

Jesus found the girl and said,

"Little one, arise!"

No food!" the disciples said.

"But this crowd needs some bread."

So Jesus did a miracle,

And everyone was fed!

Come and walk with me,"

Called Jesus from the sea.

Peter sank, and Jesus said,

"You must walk faithfully."

Jesus, please help me!"

A man cried out his plea.

Jesus touched the blind man's eyes,

And now the man could see!

$\mathcal{L}$et the children come,

They are all welcome."

Jesus said, "Be like a child

To enter God's kingdom."

Zacchaeus couldn't see

So he climbed a tree.

Jesus said, "Come down and walk

To your house with me."

Hail to the King!"

Their praises did ring.

As Jesus rode through the streets,

They waved palms of green.

$\mathcal{B}$e kind to others,

And love one another,"

Said Jesus, to teach us

To be sisters and brothers.

Jesus said, "You see

This is meant to be,

When you take the bread and wine,

Always think of me."

Jesus knelt to pray,

Saying "Take this cup away.

But Father, let your will be done.

Please do it your way!"

Even though we've sinned,

Jesus is our friend.

He gave His life for you and me,

But that was not the end!

$\mathcal{I}$n the tomb He lay...

Until the third day,

When Jesus rose from the dead!

The stone was rolled away!

$\mathcal{A}$ helper I will send,

Because I call you friends.

I go to make a place for you,

And I'll come back again!"

Little lamb,
have no fear;
Your Shepherd's
always near.
He will give you
what you need,
And fill your heart
with cheer.